Grayson's Magic Dragon

By:

Debbie L. Hepner

Illustrated By:

Marshal Uhls & James Koenig

Grayson's Magic Dragon - by Debbie L. Hepner

Copyright © 2021 by Debbie L. Hepner - www.debstories.com

Character Designs & Art Direction by James Koenig - www.freelancefridge.com

Illustrations by Marshal Uhls - www.marshaluhls.artstation.com

ISBN 978-1-7375067-4-4

All rights reserved. No portion of this book may be used or reproduced in any matter whatsoever, without written permission from the publisher. For permissions contact:

dlhepner@outlook.com

For Dallas whose remote-controlled dragon inspired this story.

And

For Grayson, our courageous 2-year-old, who with grandma's help, overcame his fear of the "Big Orange Dragon."

- DEBBIE L. HEPNER -

To my nieces & nephews, may you always find your courage and imagine BIG things!

- JAMES KOENIG -

Grayson couldn't wait to open his birthday gift from Grandma and Grandpa. He knew it would be something special. It was as though the package was calling to him. His curiosity was making his tummy flutter.

Finally when everyone was finished singing happy birthday and eating their cake and ice cream, it was time for Grayson to open his presents.

There was a new bike from Mom and Dad, a book from Aunt Sally and new pajamas from Great Grandma.

As he grabbed for the brightly colored present from Grandma and Grandpa, he thought he heard a rumble. Grayson tore open the package and came face to face with a giant orange dragon! Then he jumped as the dragon roared at him! Startled, he dropped the dragon and ran straight into Grandma's arms. Grandma hugged him and told him it was all right to be afraid, but promised the dragon would never hurt him. Grayson looked at the dragon once more, then hopped off Grandma's lap and went to ride his new bike.

Later that night when it was dark and the dragon was sitting at the bottom of his bed, Grayson inched towards it. He stared at the dragon and the dragon stared right back! Grayson reached out to touch its nose, its sharp teeth and the top of his head. It seemed to be harmless so he picked up the dragon. He was looking at its large wings as he started to pet the dragon.

Suddenly, with a **SWOOSH**, the dragon's wings started moving; steam was coming out of its nose as it gave a shy little smile. Grayson quickly covered his eyes as the dragon began to fly around the room!

Peeking through his fingers, he could see the dragon swooping around his room. He remembered Grandma's promise but he was still scared. He said to himself over and over, "The dragon will never hurt me." "The dragon will never hurt me."

The dragon landed on the bed beside him. Grayson looked at it for awhile, then gently patted the top of his head.

In a **FLASH** the bed started spinning and Grayson found himself on the back of the dragon flying high in the sky! They swooped and dived with the rush of wind in their faces. Flying was scary but Grayson kept Grandma's words in his head and slowly started laughing and enjoying the ride.

Before he knew it, the dragon started coming down from the sky. The clouds opened and Grayson could see a beautiful rainbow of candy leading to the biggest gingerbread castle he had ever seen!

The castle had frosting dripping from the roof with chocolate candy kisses on top. There were red licorice ropes holding up the drawbridge and the moat around the castle was surrounded with bubbling strawberry soda! Puffy cotton candy trees and colorful gumdrop bushes surrounded the castle. Grayson was fascinated by all the color and candy everywhere!

The dragon hovered over the castle. Grayson could see a lemon drop path, lined with lollypops, leading to gigantic root beer waterfall! The frothy root beer was cascading down an ice cream mountain with different flavored scoops of ice cream. Tiny candy sprinkles sparkled all over the ice cream mountain!

Beyond the waterfall was a chocolate pudding lake, with mini chocolate chip cookies floating on top. The lake was surrounded with colorful candy sticks… yum yum! Grayson really liked pudding!

Grayson started licking his lips and his mouth began to water. The dragon slowly swooped closer to the ground, dipped its wings and dropped him into a field of pink fluffy marshmallows.

POOF! Just as Grayson landed on the soft fluffy marshmallows, he was back in his bed staring at the dragon!

Grayson picked up his dragon and hugged him tightly. Then together they crawled under the covers and fell fast asleep.

Sweet Dreams!

Can you name Grayson's Magic Dragon?

Dragons represent – strength, power and good luck.

Some other words meaning dragon are:
Draco
Drake
Draken

ABOUT THE AUTHOR

Debbie L. Hepner

With educational degrees from Weber State University, Utah State University, and the University of Utah, Debbie taught in the Utah public school system for 30 years. Now retired from teaching, she writes children's stories. Most of her stories are inspired by experiences with her grandchildren.

Color your very own dragon, meet the author and view more books by Debbie at: www.debstories.com.

ABOUT THE ILLUSTRATORS

Marshal Uhls & James Koenig

James Koenig and Marshal Uhls have worked together on projects for many years. They originally teamed up on a large character development line with a tight deadline. They quickly discovered they enjoyed collaborating and have grown into a great team, creating spectacular books and designs together.

James has illustrated over 50 children's books and created characters and illustrations for countless other children's toys and products over the last 16 years. While he's normally the illustrator, he's had new opportunities to start writing in recent years as well.

Marshal has illustrated for video games and other products for over 11 years. He has a knack for matching the style of the characters James creates and bringing out their personalities in the books they work on together.

You can learn more about them at: **www.freelancefridge.com**.

Made in the USA
Middletown, DE
24 July 2022

69914222R00015